Annals of ENGLISH DRAMA

975-1700

A SECOND SUPPLEMENT
TO THE REVISED EDITION

S. SCHOENBAUM

Supplement one is no longer available; so if you wish a copy of it, I suggest you contact a nearby library about obtaining a photocopy.

WITH THE COMPLIMENTS

OF

S. SCHOENBAUM

The Graduate Center
The City University of New York
33 West 42nd Street
New York, New York 10036

Annals of ENGLISH DRAMA

975-1700

A SECOND SUPPLEMENT
TO THE REVISED EDITION

S. SCHOENBAUM

Department of English
NORTHWESTERN UNIVERSITY
Evanston, Illinois

Published by the Department of English
NORTHWESTERN UNIVERSITY
Evanston, Illinois

Printed in the United States of America

PREFACE

Four years have now elapsed since issuance of the first supplement to the revised *Annals*: time enough for sufficient information to accumulate to justify a second installment. Like the first, with which it is uniform in format, this supplement is distributed without charge to users of the *Annals* who have placed their names on my mailing list.

Once again I am pleased to be able to include several previously unrecorded items. The principal feature, however, is the large number of additions to the List of Editions and the List of Dissertations. For the sake of consistency (and to avoid confusion) I have cited titles in the form in which they appear in the *Annals*: *e.g.*, Bale's *King John* rather than *King Johan*, although were I to prepare another revision I think that I would now prefer *Johan*.

I have thought it well to incorporate the few items from the Addenda which I inserted as a loose page in the first number.

It is a pleasure to record my gratitude to those who have taken the trouble to forward data and queries to me: Clive Burch, Elizabeth Story Donno, Mrs. V. J. Edden, Philip Edwards, E. Gillett, Alfred Harbage, Theodore Hofmann, William Ingram, Stanley J. Kahrl, J. C. Maxwell, J. C. Meagher, John Murphy, Catharine Regan, D. F. Rowan, John H. Smith, Miss S. D. Thomson, Eleanor Withington, and Laetitia Yeandle. To Mrs. Margaret Buth I am grateful for her careful typing of this supplement.

I would be very grateful indeed to hear from any scholars who have noticed errors, in the *Annals* or these supplements, or who can furnish new items of information. Such data will be invaluable for the third supplement.

S.S.
21 October 1970

CORRECTIONS AND ADDITIONS

I. INTRODUCTION

P. xiii. To *Sources of the Information* add F. P. Wilson, *The English Drama 1485-1585*, ed. G. K. Hunter, 1969.

II. CHRONOLOGY AND INFORMATION

Fifteenth century (pp. 12-13). *Add entire entry:* Author: Anon. Title: *Corpus Christi Play*. Limits: 1478, 1482 (ment.) Type: Mystery. Auspices: Stamford, Lincolnshire. Earliest Texts: Lost.

Fifteenth century (pp. 14-15). To 'lost plays of traditional character mentioned at various times after 1495' add *Noah Play* (ment. 1518-1519, Boston, Lincolnshire: sponsored by St. Mary's Guild); *Corpus Christi Play* (ment. 1519-1520 and later, Louth, Lincolnshire); *Holy John of Bower Play* (1527, Grimsby: sponsored by Mariners' Guild?).

1503. *The Welcome for Princess Margaret*. Earliest Texts: add MS (descrip.). Last Ed.: add 1774. [See J. Leland, *Collectanea*, ed. T. Hearne (London, 1774), IV, 288ff.]

1520. 'Summer and Lust', etc. Limits: for 1520 read 1519. Transfer entire entry to 1519.

1537. *Albion Knight*. Limits: for *c*. 1537-1566 read *c*. 1537-1565.

1545. *Add entire entry:* Author: Foxe, John. Title: *Titus et Gesippus*. Limits: 1544-1545. Type: Latin Comedy. Auspices: Unacted. Earliest Text: MS. [See J. H. Smith, 'Sempronia, John Lyly, and John Foxe's Comedy of *Titus and Gesippus*', *PQ*, XLVIII (1969), 554-61.]

1550. *Somebody, Avarice, and Minister*. Title: add (Trans. *La Vérité cachée*.)

1553. *Add entire entry:* Author: Anon. Title: *Queen Mary's Entry into London*. Limits: 30 Sept. Type: Royal Reception. Auspices: London. Earliest Texts: MS (descrip.). Last Ed.: 1850.

[See *The Chronicle of Queen Jane, and of Two Years of Queen Mary . . .*, ed. J. G. Nichols (London, 1850), pp. 27-30 (Camden Soc. Pub's., Vol. XLVIII).]

1562. *Gorboduc*. Limits: for 28 Jan. read 6 Jan.

1579. *A Marriage between Wit and Wisdom*. Author: for Merbury, Francis read Merbury, Francis (?).

1582. *Bellum Grammaticale*. Author: for Hutton, Leonard read Hutton, Leonard (?).

1582. *Add entire entry:*
Author: Anon. Title: *A Virgin Play*. Limits: 22 Feb. (acted). Type: Unknown. Auspices: Unknown. Earliest Texts: Lost. [See *Diary of Richard Madox*, Brit. Mus. Cotton MS. App. XLVII, f. 6^v.]

1585. *Gallathea*. Title: for (*Titirus and Galathea*, S.R., 1585?) read (*Titirus and Galathea*, S.R., 1585). Limits: for 1584-1588 read 1583-1585.

1587. *Alphonsus, King of Aragon*. Auspices: for Unknown read Queen's (?). [See G. M. Pinciss, 'Thomas Creede and the Repertory of the Queen's Men', *MP*, LVII (1970), 321-30.]

1587. *The Spanish Tragedy*. Author: for Kyd, T. (revised by Jonson, B.) read Kyd, T. (lost additions by Jonson, B.).

1587. *The Love of King David and Fair Bethsabe*. Limits: add (Composition 'sometime during the winter and spring of 1593/4' recently advocated). [See Peele, *Dramatic Works*, gen. ed. C. T. Prouty (1952-70), III, 143.]

1588. *The Wounds of Civil War, or Marius and Scilla*. Limits: for 1587-1592 read 1586-1592.

1588. *The Wars of Cyrus*. Author: add (Farrant, R.?). Limits: for 1587-1594 read 1576-1580 or a. 1587.

1591. *Locrine*. Auspices: for Unknown read Queen's (?). [See Pinciss, 'Thomas Creede and the Repertory of the Queen's Men', 321-30.]

1591. *Locrine*. Last Ed.: for 1908G read 1908^{91}(G).

1592. *Summer's Last Will and Testament*. Title: add (Expansion of entertainment written by Lyly for Queen's progress in 1591?). [See M. R. Best, 'Nashe, Lyly, and *Summers Last Will and Testament*', *PQ*, XLVIII (1969), 1-11.]

1599. Addenda. *Don Horatio*. Author: add (Kyd, T.?). Title: add (Same as *I Jeronimo, with the Wars of Portugal*, 1604?). Earliest Texts: for Lost read Lost (?). [See T. Kyd, *The First Part of Hieronimo and The Spanish Tragedy*, ed. A. S. Cairncross (Lincoln, Neb., 1967), pp. xiii-xix; also A. Freeman, *Thomas Kyd* (Oxford, 1967), pp. 175-77.]

1602. *Sir Giles Goosecap*. Auspices: for Chapel read Chapel (?).

1604. *I Jeronimo, with the Wars of Portugal*. Author: add (Kyd, T.?). Title: add (Bad Quarto or revision of *Don Horatio*, 1599 Addenda?). Auspices: for King's (?) read King's (?) Chapel (?). [See Kyd, *The First Part of Hieronimo and The Spanish Tragedy*, ed. Cairncross, pp. xiii-xix; also Freeman, *Thomas Kyd*, pp. 175-77.]

1605. *Alba, or Vertumnus*. Title: for *Alba, or Vertumnus* read *Alba*. [See R. L. Nochimson, 'Robert Burton's Authorship of *Alba*: A Lost Letter Recovered', *R.E.S.*, N.S., XXI (1970), 325-31.]

1607. *The Entertainment at Theobalds*. Earliest Texts: for 1616 read 1616 & MS.

1608. *Add entire entry:*
Author: Jonson, Ben. Title: *The Entertainment at Salisbury House for James I*. Limits: 5-11 May. Type: Royal Entertainment. Auspices: Host: Earl of Salisbury. Earliest Texts: Lost. [See S. McMillin, 'Jonson's Early Entertainments: New Information from Hatfield House', *Renaissance Drama*, N.S., I (1968), 153-66.]

1609. *Add entire entry:*
Author: Jonson, Ben. Title: *The Entertainment at Britain's Burse for James I*. Limits: 11 April. Type: Royal Entertainment. Auspices: Host: Earl of Salisbury. Earliest Texts: Lost. [See McMillin, 'Jonson's Early Entertainments', pp. 153-66.]

1611. *A Chaste Maid in Cheapside*. Limits: for 1611-1613 read 1613. Transfer entire entry to 1613.

1613. *The Mask of the Middle Temple and Lincoln's Inn*. Title: add *(The Memorable Mask)*.

1613. *No Wit, No Help Like a Woman's*. Limits: 1611-1612. Transfer entire entry to 1612. [See David George, 'Weather-Wise's Almanac and the Date of Middleton's "No Wit No Help Like a Woman's"', *N&Q*, CCXI (1966), 297-301.]

1615. *The Guise*. Title: for *The Guise* read *Guise*. Type: for Tragedy (?) read Comedy (?). [See R. G. Howarth, 'Webster's "Guise"', *N&Q*, CCXI (1966), 294-96.]

1621. *A New Way to Pay Old Debts*. Limits: for 1621-1625 read 1625. Auspices: for Red Bull Company (?) (later Queen Henrietta's) read Queen Henrietta's. Transfer entire entry to 1625.

1633. *Perkin Warbeck*. Limits: for *c*. 1629-1634 read *c*. 1625-1634.

1635. *King Free-Will.* Earliest Texts: for 1635* or MS (lost) read MS (lost?).

1638. *The Constant Maid.* Title: for *The Constant Maid, or Love Will Find out the Way* read *The Constant Maid (Love Will Find out the Way).* Limits: for 1626 (?)-1640 read *c.* 1630-1640 (originally written but not acted in *c.* 1630, and revised 1636-1640?). [See A. P. Reimer, 'Shirley's Revisions and the Date of *The Constant Maid*', *R.E.S.*, N.S., XVII (1966), 141-48.]

1641. *Add entire entry:*
Author: Taylor, John. Title: *A Pedlar and a Romish Priest.* Limits: 1641. Type: Polemical Religious Dialogue. Auspices: Closet. Earliest Texts: 1641*.

1642. *Add entire entry:*
Author: Anon. Title: *A Threefold Discourse between Three Neighbours, Algate, Bishopsgate, and John Heyden the Late Cobler of Houndsditch, a Professed Brownist.* Limits: 1642. Type: Political Dialogue. Auspices: Closet. Earliest Texts: 1642*.

1642. *Add entire entry:*
Author: Anon. (Tatham, J. ?). Title: *The Copt-Hall Interlude.* Limits: 1642. Auspices: Unknown. Earliest Texts: MS.

1646. *Add entire entry:*
Author: Llewellyn, Martin ('Mr. Loyd' on t.p.). Title: *The King Found at Southwell.* Limits: 5 May. Type: Entertainment. Auspices: Cavaliers at Oxford. Earliest Texts: 1646*F. [See J. P. Cutts, 'The Dramatic Writing of Martin Llewellyn', *PQ*, XLVII (1968), 16-29.]

1648. *A Key to the Cabinet of the Parliament.* Non-dramatic; delete entire entry.

1656. *Add entire entry:*
Author: Anon. Title: 'Prodigality and Covetousness'. Type: Moral Interlude (?). Limits: 31 Jan. (acted). Auspices: Schoolchildren in Forres. Earliest Texts: Lost. [See *Diary of Alexander Brodie and of his Son, James Brodie* (1863), p. 173; cited by T. Tobin, 'School Plays in Scotland, 1656-1693', *SCN*, XXVII (1969), 49.]

1661. *Add entire entry:*
Author: 'J.C.' Title: *A New Fiction, As We Were: A.I.M.E.I.M.I.D2.F.4.* Type: Political Allegory. Auspices: Closet. Earliest Texts: 1661*.

1690. *Add entire entry:*
Author: Anon. Title: *The Mystery of Iniquity, or The Revolu-*

tion, Deduced to the Time of K. J. His Being Forced . . . to Retire from England. Limits: *c.* 1690. Type: Political Play. Auspices: Closet. Earliest Texts: MS.

III. SUPPLEMENTARY LIST I

P. 202. *Add entire entry:*
Death. A Comedy. By Robert Squire. Trans. Drury's *Mors Comoedia.* First half 17th cent. MS.

P. 203. *Add entire entry:*
The Twice Changed Friar. Anon. comedy, *'temp. Charles I'.* Ment. (by Bullen?) as extant in 'a seventeenth-century MS. volume from a Warwickshire library'. [See Anon., *'"The Twice chang'd friar. A comedie"', The Gentleman's Magazine,* CCC (1906), 285-90.]

P. 204. *Add entire entry:*
Christmas pageant, 1565, performed at Lincoln. Speakers are three Senators. MS. in Registers of Corporation of Lincoln, Vol. IV, flyleaf (printed in *Hist. MSS. Comm.*, 14th Report, Appendix, Pt. VIII [1895], pp. 58-60).

P. 204. *Add entire entry:*
A Speech of 'Delight', extract, late 15th cent., from a morality. Bodl. MS. Tanner 407, ff. 43^v-44. [See *Non-Cycle Plays and Fragments*, ed. N. Davis (Oxford, 1970), pp. cxx-cxxiii, 121-22.]

IV. SUPPLEMENTARY LIST II

P. 208. *Add entire entry:*
The following items are bound into Vol. III of the Family Letters of Sir William Herrick (1562-1653): Introd. by 'pore amintas' to 'square play' performed by 'shepherd boys', *c.* 1570-90; Prol. introducing maskers dressed as sailors for a wedding mask, *c.* 1570-90. [See J. G. Nichols, 'An Elizabethan Marriage', *N&Q*, 2nd Ser., X (1860), 101-2; also Hofmann & Freeman Catalogue 25, Oct. 1968. Latter contains facsimile of first item.]

V. INDEX OF ENGLISH PLAYWRIGHTS

P. 222. Foxe, John. Add 1545.

P. 223. Haynes, Joe. For 1648 read *c.* 1648. [See K. M. Cameron, 'Jo Haynes, *Infamis*', *Theatre Notebook*, XXIV (1969/70), 56-67.]

P. 224. Hughes, Thomas. For d. a. 1618 read d. a. 1623.
P. 225. Add: Llewellyn, or Lluelyn, Martin (1616-1681: physician), 1646 Supp. II.
P. 226. For Penroodock, or Penrudock, William read Penroodock, or Penrudock, John.
P. 227. Rowley, Samuel. For d. a. 1624 read d. 1624. [See J. A. Somerset, 'New Facts Concerning Samuel Rowley', *R.E.S.*, N.S., XVII (1966), 293-97.]
P. 229. Add: Squire, Robert (Unknown), Supplementary List I (Supp. II).

VI. INDEX OF ENGLISH PLAYS

P. 288. For Venus, the White Tragedy or the Green Knight (by Philips), *mentioned* 1599 *by Nashe in* Lenten Stuff, *and possibly a play or plays* read The White Tragedy or the Green Knight, *mentioned* 1599 *by Nashe in* Lenten Stuff, *and possibly a play or plays*. Transfer entry to p. 290. ['Philips his Venus', referred to by Nashe, is non-dramatic (*Philippes Venus*, 1591, by 'Io.M.'); see T. Nashe, *Works*, ed. R. B. McKerrow (Oxford, 1958), IV, 413.]

VII. LIST OF THEATRES

P. 304. NEWINGTON BUTTS. Add: [The unknown builder has been identified as Richard Hickes, a Yeoman of the Queen's Guard and the leaseholder of the property on which the playhouse was built; see I. Darlington, *St George's Fields, The Survey of London*, XXV (London County Council, 1955), 86. The builder may, however, have been Hickes's tenant, Jerome Savage, a player with Warwick's Men, and the playhouse was possibly erected as early as 1576, and first occupied by Warwick's company; see W. Ingram, 'The Playhouse at Newington Butts: A New Proposal', forthcoming in *Shakespeare Quarterly*, Autumn 1970.]

VIII. APPENDIX

P. 310. Glapthorne, Henry. *The Lady Mother*. For ff. 212-45 read ff. 186-211.
P. 310. Foxe, John. *Christus Triumphans*. For Brit. Mus. MS. Lansdowne 1073 read Brit. Mus. MS. Lansdowne 1045. Add, under Foxe, the following entry:
Titus et Gesippus (L). Brit. Mus. MS. Lansdowne 388,

ff. 121^r-46^r, 112^r-16^v (pages out of sequence).
P. 312. Jonson, Ben. Add: *The Entertainment at Theobalds*. Folger Shakespeare Library MS. X.d.475.
P. 316. *Add entire entry:*
SQUIRE, ROBERT
Death. A Comedy. Newberry Lib. Case MS. 5A.7.
P. 316. *Abraham and Isaac (Brome).* For present entry substitute: MS, *The Book of Brome*, ff. 15-22, formerly at Brome Manor, Suffolk; now in the Beinecke Rare Book and Manuscript Library of Yale University. [See Thomas E. Marston, 'The Book of Brome', *The Yale University Library Gazette*, XLI (1967), 141-45.]
P. 317. *The Copt-Hall Interlude*. MS. D/DWZ in Essex Record Office.
P. 318. *Free-Will*. Add: [Note in MS reads: 'This was Copied (from the Old Morality printed in the black letter,) by Francis Bristowe, Gent., in 1635'. See Supp. I, p. 12.]
P. 319. Add: *The Mystery of Iniquity*. National Lib. of Scotland MS. 2093, ff. 1-26.
P. 319. *The Pride of Life*. Add: Lost by fire in 1922.
P. 320. Add: *Queen Mary's Entry into London*. Brit. Mus. MS. Harleian 194.

IX. LIST OF EDITIONS

[The following editions have been published since the appearance of the first supplement.]

A. COLLECTIONS

Beaumont, Francis, and John Fletcher. *Dramatic Works*, gen. ed. F. Bowers. Vol. I. Cambridge, 1966. Comprises *The Knight of the Burning Pestle* (ed. C. Hoy), *The Mask of the Inner Temple and Gray's Inn* (ed. F. Bowers), *The Woman Hater* (ed. G. W. Williams), *The Coxcomb* (ed. I. B. Cauthen, Jr.), *Philaster* (ed. R. K. Turner), and *The Captain* (ed. L. A. Beaurline). Vol. II. Cambridge, 1970. Contains *The Maid's Tragedy* (ed. R. K. Turner), *A King and No King* (ed. G. W. Williams), *Cupid's Revenge* (ed. F. Bowers), *The Scornful Lady* (ed. C. Hoy), and *Love's Pilgrimage* (ed. L. A. Beaurline).
A Book of Masques, gen. eds. T. J. B. Spencer and S. W. Wells. Cambridge, 1967. Contains *The Vision of the Twelve Goddesses* (ed. J. Rees), *Oberon, the Fairy Prince* (ed. R.

Hosley), *Love Freed from Ignorance and Folly* (ed. N. Sanders), *The Lords' Mask* (ed. I. A. Shapiro), *The Mask of the Inner Temple and Gray's Inn* (ed. P. Edwards), *The Mask of Flowers* (ed. E. A. J. Honigmann), *The Mask of the Inner Temple (Ulysses and Circe)* (ed. R. F. Hill), *Lovers Made Men* (ed. S. Wells), *Pleasure Reconciled to Virtue* (ed. R. A. Foakes), *The Inner Temple Mask, or Mask of Heroes* (ed. R. C. Bald), *The Triumph of Peace* (ed. C. Leech), *The Spring's Glory* (ed. J. R. Brown), *Salmacida Spolia* (ed. T. J. B. Spencer), and *Cupid and Death* (ed. B. A. Harris).

Campion, Thomas. *Works*, ed. W. R. Davis. New York, 1967. Includes *The Mask at Lord Hay's Marriage, The Lords' Mask,* and *The Mask at the Earl of Somerset's Marriage*.

Chapman, George. *Plays*, gen. ed. A. Holaday, assisted by M. Kiernan. Vol. I: *The Comedies*. Urbana, Ill., 1970. Comprises *The Blind Beggar of Alexandria* (ed. L. E. Berry), *An Humorous Day's Mirth* (ed. A. Holaday), *The Gentleman Usher* (ed. R. Ornstein), *All Fools* (ed. G. B. Evans), *May Day* (ed. R. F. Welsh), *Monsieur D'Olive* (ed. A. Holaday), *The Widow's Tears* (ed. R. Ornstein), and *The Mask of the Middle Temple and Lincoln's Inn* (ed. G. B. Evans).

Congreve, William. *Complete Works*, ed. H. Davis. Chicago, 1967. (Curtain Playwrights.) Contains *The Double Dealer, The Old Bachelor, Love for Love, The Mourning Bride,* and *The Way of the World.*

Dryden, John. *Four Comedies*, ed. L. A. Beaurline and F. Bowers. Chicago, 1967. (Curtain Playwrights.) Consists of *Sir Martin Mar-all, An Evening's Love, Secret Love,* and *Marriage à la Mode.*

________. *Four Tragedies*, ed. L. A. Beaurline and F. Bowers. Chicago, 1967. (Curtain Playwrights.) Consists of *All for Love, Aureng-Zebe, Don Sebastian,* and *The Indian Emperor.*

________. *Works*, ed. H. T. Swedenberg, Jr. (gen. ed.). Berkeley and Los Angeles, 1966. Vol. IX, ed. J. Loftis and V. A. Dearing. Consists of *The Indian Emperor, Secret Love,* and *Sir Martin Mar-all.* [N.B. Announced for publication in November, 1970, is Vol. X, ed. M. E. Novak and G. R. Guffey, comprising *The Tempest, Tyrannic Love,* and *An Evening's Love.*]

Jonson, Ben. *The Complete Masques*, ed. S. Orgel. New Haven and London, 1969. (Yale Ben Jonson.) Contains *The Mask of Blackness; The Mask of Beauty; Hymenaei; The Mask at*

Lord Haddington's Marriage; The Mask of Queens; Prince Henry's Barriers; Oberon, the Fairy Prince; Love Freed from Ignorance and Folly; Love Restored; A Challenge at Tilt; The Irish Mask; Mercury Vindicated from the Alchemists at Court; The Golden Age Restored; Christmas His Mask; The Vision of Delight; Lovers Made Men; Pleasure Reconciled to Virtue; For the Honour of Wales; News from the New World Discovered in the Moon; Pan's Anniversary, or The Shepherds' Holiday; The Gypsies Metamorphosed; The Mask of Augurs; Time Vindicated to Himself and to His Honours; Neptune's Triumph for the Return of Albion; The Mask of Owls; The Fortunate Isles and Their Union; Love's Triumph through Callipolis; and *Chloridia: Rites to Chloris and Her Nymphs.*

Knevet, Ralph. *Shorter Poems*, ed. A. M. Charles. Columbus, Ohio, 1966. Includes *Rhodon and Iris.*

The Macro Plays, ed. M. Eccles. Oxford, 1969. (Early English Text Soc.) Contains *The Castle of Perseverance, Wisdom,* and *Mankind.*

Non-Cycle Plays and Fragments, ed. N. Davis. Oxford, 1970. (Early English Text Soc.) Contains *Shrewsbury Fragments, Norwich Grocers' Play, Newcastle Play (Noah's Ark), Abraham and Isaac* (Dublin), *Abraham and Isaac* (Brome), *The Play of the Sacrament, The Pride of Life, Dux Moraud,* 'The Cambridge Prologue' [see *Annals*, 'An English Mystery Play Fragment Ante 1300', p. 204], *Bury St Edmunds Fragment*, 'The Durham Prologue' [see *Annals*, 'Prol., 15th cent. . . .', p. 203], 'The Ashmole Fragment' [see *Annals*, 'A Dramatic Fragment from a Caesar Augustus Play', p. 203], 'The Reynes Extracts' [see above, p. 5, 'A Speech of "Delight"', and *Annals*, 'A Sixteenth Century English Mystery Fragment', p. 203].

Peele, George. *Dramatic Works*, gen. ed. C. T. Prouty. New Haven and London, 1970. Vol. III. Consists of *The Arraignment of Paris*, ed. R. M. Benbow; *The Love of King David and Fair Bethsabe*, ed. E. Blistein; and *The Old Wives Tale*, ed. F. S. Hook.

Wycherley, William. *Complete Plays*, ed. G. Weales. New York, 1966. (The Stuart Editions.) Comprises *Love in a Wood, The Gentleman Dancing-Master, The Country Wife,* and *The Plain Dealer.*

B. INDIVIDUAL PLAYS

[Note: In Great Britain the Fountainwell Drama Texts are published by Oliver and Boyd, Edinburgh; the Regents series, by Edward Arnold, London. Publication dates of British editions may differ from the American.]

Bacon (?); Campion; Davison; etc. *Gesta Grayorum*, ed. D. S. Bland. Liverpool, 1968. (English Reprints Series.)

Bale, John. *I and II King John*, ed. B. B. Adams. San Marino, Calif., 1969.

Beaumont, Francis. *The Knight of the Burning Pestle*, ed. J. Doebler. Lincoln, Neb., 1967. (Regents Renaissance Drama Ser.)

________. *The Knight of the Burning Pestle*, ed. A. Gurr. Berkeley and Los Angeles, 1968. (Fountainwell Drama Texts.)

________. *The Knight of the Burning Pestle*, ed. M. Hattaway. London, 1969.

________; Fletcher, J. *The Maid's Tragedy*, ed. H. B. Norland. Lincoln, Neb., 1968. (Regents Renaissance Drama Ser.)

________. *The Maid's Tragedy*, ed. A. Gurr. Berkeley and Los Angeles, 1969. (Fountainwell Drama Texts.)

________. *Philaster*, ed. A. Gurr. London, 1969. (Revels Plays.)

Behn, Aphra. *I The Rover*, ed. F. Link. Lincoln, Neb., 1967. (Regents Restoration Drama Ser.)

Brome, Richard. *The Antipodes*, ed. A. Haaker. Lincoln, Neb., 1966. (Regents Renaissance Drama Ser.)

________. *A Jovial Crew*, ed. A. Haaker. Lincoln, Neb., 1968. (Regents Renaissance Drama Ser.)

Chapman, George. *All Fools*, ed. F. Manley. Lincoln, Neb., 1968. (Regents Renaissance Drama Ser.)

________. *The Gentleman Usher*, ed. J. H. Smith. Lincoln, Neb., 1970. (Regents Renaissance Drama Ser.)

________. *The Widow's Tears*, ed. E. M. Smeak. Lincoln, Neb., 1966. (Regents Renaissance Drama Ser.)

Chettle, H.; Munday, A. *The Death of Robert, Earl of Huntingdon*, ed. J. C. Meagher. Oxford, 1965(1967). (Malone Society Reprints.)

Clyomon and Clamydes, ed. B. J. Littleton. The Hague, 1968.

Congreve, William. *Love for Love*, ed. E. L. Avery. Lincoln, Neb., 1966. (Regents Restoration Drama Ser.)

Congreve, William. *Love for Love*, ed. A. N. Jeffares. London, 1967.
________. *Love for Love*, ed. M. M. Kelsall. London, 1969. (The New Mermaids.)
Crowne, John. *City Politiques*, ed. J. H. Wilson. Lincoln, Neb., 1967. (Regents Restoration Drama Ser.)
________. *Sir Courtly Nice*, ed. C. B. Hughes. The Hague, 1967.
Dekker, Thomas. *The Shoemakers' Holiday*, ed. P. C. Davies. Berkeley and Los Angeles, 1968. (Fountainwell Drama Texts.)
Etherege, George. *The Man of Mode*, ed. W. B. Carnochan. Lincoln, Neb., 1966. (Regents Restoration Drama Ser.)
Field, N.; Massinger, P. *The Fatal Dowry*, ed. T. A. Dunn. Berkeley and Los Angeles, 1969. (Fountainwell Drama Texts.)
Fletcher, John. *The Woman's Prize*, ed. G. B. Ferguson. The Hague, 1966.
________ (with Massinger, P.?). *Beggars' Bush*, ed. J. H. Dorenkamp. The Hague, 1968.
Ford, John. *The Broken Heart*, ed. D. K. Anderson, Jr. Lincoln, Neb., 1968. (Regents Renaissance Drama Ser.)
________. *Perkin Warbeck*, ed. P. Ure. London, 1968. (Revels Plays.)
________. *'Tis Pity She's a Whore*, ed. N. W. Bawcutt. Lincoln, Neb., 1966. (Regents Renaissance Drama Ser.)
________. *'Tis Pity She's a Whore*, ed. B. Morris. London, 1968. (The New Mermaids.)
Greene, Robert. *Friar Bacon and Friar Bungay*, ed. J. A. Lavin. London, 1969. (The New Mermaids.)
________. *The Scottish History of James IV*, ed. J. A. Lavin. London, 1967. (The New Mermaids.)
________. *The Scottish History of James IV*, ed. N. Sanders. London, 1970. (Revels Plays.)
Heywood, Thomas. *I and II The Fair Maid of the West*, ed. R. K. Turner, Jr. Lincoln, Neb., 1967. (Regents Renaissance Drama Ser.)
I Jeronimo, with the Wars of Portugal, in T. Kyd, *The First Part of Hieronimo and The Spanish Tragedy*, ed. A. S. Cairncross. Lincoln, Neb., 1967. (Regents Renaissance Drama Ser.)
Jonson, Ben. *The Alchemist*, ed. F. H. Mares. London, 1967. (Revels Plays.)
________. *The Alchemist*, ed. J. B. Steane. London, 1967.
________. *The Alchemist*, ed. S. Musgrove. Berkeley and Los Angeles, 1968. (Fountainwell Drama Texts.)

Jonson, Ben. *Epicoene, or The Silent Woman*, ed. L. A. Beaurline. Lincoln, Neb., 1966. (Regents Renaissance Drama Ser.)

________. *Every Man in His Humour*, ed. M. Seymour Smith. London, 1967. (The New Mermaids.)

________. *Every Man in His Humour*, ed. G. B. Jackson. New Haven and London, 1970. (Yale Ben Jonson.)

________. *Sejanus His Fall*, ed. J. A. Barish. New Haven, 1965. (Yale Ben Jonson.)

________. *Volpone*, ed. J. L. Halio. Berkeley and Los Angeles, 1968. (Fountainwell Drama Texts.)

________. *Volpone*, ed. P. Brockbank. London, 1969. (The New Mermaids.)

Kyd, Thomas. *The Spanish Tragedy*, in *The First Part of Hieronimo and The Spanish Tragedy*, ed. A. S. Cairncross. Lincoln, Neb., 1967. (Regents Renaissance Drama Ser.)

________. *The Spanish Tragedy*, ed. T. W. Ross. Berkeley and Los Angeles, 1968. (Fountainwell Drama Texts.)

________. *The Spanish Tragedy*, ed. J. R. Mulryne. London, 1970. (The New Mermaids.)

Lee, Nathaniel. *Lucius Junius Brutus, Father of His Country*, ed. J. Loftis. Lincoln, Neb., 1967. (Regents Restoration Drama Ser.)

Lodge, Thomas. *The Wounds of Civil War*, ed. J. W. Houppert. Lincoln, Neb., 1969. (Regents Renaissance Drama Ser.)

Lyly, John. *Gallathea* and *Midas*, ed. A. B. Lancashire. Lincoln, Neb., 1969. (Regents Renaissance Drama Ser.)

Marlowe, Christopher. *Dido, Queen of Carthage* and *The Massacre at Paris*, ed. H. J. Oliver. London, 1968. (Revels Plays.)

________. *Edward II*, ed. W. M. Merchant. London, 1967. (The New Mermaids.)

________. *The Jew of Malta*, ed. T. W. Craik. London, 1966. (The New Mermaids.)

________. *I and II Tamburlaine the Great*, ed. J. D. Jump. Lincoln, Neb., 1967. (Regents Renaissance Drama Ser.)

Marston, John. *The Dutch Courtesan*, ed. P. Davison. Berkeley and Los Angeles, 1968. (Fountainwell Drama Texts.)

________. *The Malcontent*, ed. B. Harris. London, 1967. (The New Mermaids.)

Middleton, Thomas. *A Chaste Maid in Cheapside*, ed. A. Brissenden. London, 1968. (The New Mermaids.)

________. *A Chaste Maid in Cheapside*, ed. R. B. Parker. London, 1969. (Revels Plays.)

Middleton, Thomas. *A Chaste Maid in Cheapside*, ed. C. Barber. Berkeley and Los Angeles, 1969. (Fountainwell Drama Texts.)
_______. *A Game at Chess*, ed. J. W. Harper. London, 1966. (The New Mermaids.)
_______. *Michaelmas Term*, ed. R. Levin. Lincoln, Neb., 1966. (Regents Renaissance Drama Ser.)
_______. *A Trick to Catch the Old One*, ed. C. Barber. Berkeley and Los Angeles, 1968. (Fountainwell Drama Texts.)
_______. *A Trick to Catch the Old One*, ed. G. J. Watson. London, 1969. (The New Mermaids.)
_______. *Women Beware Women*, ed. R. Gill. London, 1968. (The New Mermaids.)
_______; Rowley, W. *The Changeling*, ed. G. W. Williams. Lincoln, Neb., 1966. (Regents Renaissance Drama Ser.)
Norton, T.; Sackville, T. *Gorboduc*, ed. I. B. Cauthen, Jr. Lincoln, Neb., 1970. (Regents Renaissance Drama Ser.)
Origo Mundi; Passio Domini; Resurrexio Domini, trans. M. Harris, as *The Cornish Ordinalia: A Medieval Dramatic Trilogy*. Washington, D.C., 1969.
Otway, Thomas. *Venice Preserved*, ed. M. M. Kelsall. Lincoln, Neb., 1969. (Regents Restoration Drama Ser.)
The Revenger's Tragedy, ed. L. J. Ross. Lincoln, Neb., 1966. (Regents Renaissance Drama Ser.)
The Revenger's Tragedy, ed. B. Gibbons. London, 1967. (The New Mermaids.)
Shakespeare; Fletcher (& Beaumont?). *The Two Noble Kinsmen*, ed. G. R. Proudfoot. Lincoln, Neb., 1970. (Regents Renaissance Drama Ser.)
Sidney, Sir Philip. *The Lady of May*, ed. R. Kimbrough and P. Murphy. 'The Helmingham Hall Manuscript of Sidney's *The Lady of May*: A Commentary and Transcription', *Renaissance Drama*, N.S., I (1968), 103-19.
Swetnam the Woman-Hater Arraigned by Women, ed. C. Crandyll. Lafayette, Ind., 1969. (Purdue Univ. Studies.)
Wager, W. *The Longer Thou Livest the More Fool Thou Art* and *Enough Is as Good as a Feast*, ed. R. M. Benbow. Lincoln, Neb., 1967. (Regents Renaissance Drama Ser.)
Webster, John. *The White Devil*, ed. J. R. Mulryne. Lincoln, Neb., 1969. (Regents Renaissance Drama Ser.)
_______. *The White Devil*, ed. C. Hart. Berkeley and Los Angeles, 1970. (Fountainwell Drama Texts.)
Wycherley, William. *The Plain Dealer*, ed. L. Hughes. Lincoln, Neb., 1967. (Regents Restoration Drama Ser.)

C. FACSIMILES

[The date of the edition reproduced is supplied in round brackets.]

Benjamin Blom:

Killigrew, Thomas. *Comedies and Tragedies* (1664). Consists of *The Princess, The Parson's Wedding, The Pilgrim, I and II Cicilia and Clorinda, Thomaso, I and II Bellamira Her Dream, Claracilla,* and *The Prisoners.*

Cornmarket Press:

Betterton, Thomas. *Henry IV, with the Humours of Sir John Falstaff* (1700).
Boyle, Roger. *Henry V* (1668).
________. *Mustapha, Son of Solyman the Magnificent* (1668).
Cibber, Colley. *Richard III* ([1700]).
Crowne, John. *Henry VI, the First Part, with the Murder of Humphrey Duke of Gloucester* (1681).
________. *The Misery of Civil War* (1680).
Davenant, William. *Macbeth* (1674).
________; Dryden, J. *The Tempest, or The Enchanted Island* (1670).
Dryden, John. *Troilus and Cressida, or Truth Found Too Late* (1679).
Gildon, Charles. *Measure for Measure, or Beauty the Best Advocate* (1700).
Lacy, John. *Sauny the Scot, or The Taming of the Shrew* (1698).
Otway, Thomas. *Caius Marius* (1680).
Ravenscroft, Edward. *Titus Andronicus, or The Rape of Lavinia* (1687).
Sedley, Charles. *Antony and Cleopatra* (1677).
Settle, Elkanah (?). *The Fairy Queen* (1692).
Shadwell, Thomas. *Timon of Athens, the Man-Hater* (1678).
Shadwell, T. (?) (& Betterton, T. ?). *The Tempest, or the Enchanted Island* (1674).
Tate, Nahum. *The Ingratitude of a Commonwealth, or The Fall of Caius Martius Coriolanus* (1682).
________. *King Lear* (1681).
________. *Richard II* (1681).

Scolar Press:

Chapman, George. *The Revenge of Bussy D'Ambois* (1613).

Congreve, William. *Love for Love* (1695).
________. *The Way of the World* (1700).
Dryden, John. *All for Love* (1678).
Ford, John. *'Tis Pity She's a Whore* (1633).
Jonson, Ben. *Volpone* (1607).
Kyd, Thomas. *The Spanish Tragedy* (1592).
Marlowe, Christopher. *Doctor Faustus* (1604, 1616).
________. *The Jew of Malta* (1633).
Marston, John. *The Malcontent* (1604).
Massinger, Philip. *A New Way to Pay Old Debts* (1633).
Middleton, Thomas. *A Chaste Maid in Cheapside* (1630).
________. *A Trick to Catch the Old One* (1607).
Norton, T.; Sackville, T. *Gorboduc* (1570).
Peele, George. *The Old Wives Tale* (1595).
Shakespeare, William. *Hamlet* (1603, 1605, 1623).
Shirley, James. *The Triumph of Beauty*. In *Poems* (1646).
Tourneur, Cyril. *The Atheist's Tragedy* (1611).
Webster, John. *The Duchess of Malfi* (1623).
Wycherley, William. *The Country Wife* (1675).

Theatrum Orbis Terrarum (Amsterdam) and De Capo Press (New York):
Beaumont, Francis. *The Knight of the Burning Pestle* (1613).
________, with Fletcher, J. *Philaster, or Love Lies a-Bleeding* (1620).
Fletcher (with Massinger?; Jonson?; & another?). *The Bloody Brother* (1639).
Lindsay, Sir David. *A Satire of the Three Estates* (1602).
Seneca His Ten Tragedies, Translated into English (1581).

X. LIST OF DISSERTATIONS

Alphonsus, King of Aragon, ed. M. J. Sulzman (St. Louis Univ., 1968).
The Ball, ed. D. G. McKinnon (Univ. of Illinois, 1965).
The Brazen Age, ed. R. M. Cacciola (Vanderbilt Univ., 1969).
The Bugbears, ed. J. D. Clark (Univ. of Arizona, 1967).
Calisto, ed. [as *The Escapes of Jupiter*] by H. D. Janzen (Wayne State Univ., 1969).
Cambyses, King of Persia, ed. R. M. Barsam (Univ. of Southern California, 1967).
Claudius Tiberius Nero, ed. J. F. Abbick (Univ. of North Carolina, 1967).
The City Madam, ed. P. H. Farrier (Univ. of Virginia, 1929).

Cleopatra (Daniel), ed. H. L. Sampson (St. Louis Univ., 1966).
The Conspiracy and Tragedy of Charles Duke of Byron, ed. G. W. Ray III (Univ. of Rochester, 1966).
The Courageous Turk, or Amurath I, ed. D. Carnegie (Univ. Coll., London, 1967). [In *A Critical Edition of the Turkish Tragedies of Thomas Goffe*.]
Dido (Gager), ed. and trans. H. B. Schramm, in *William Gager and the Dido Tradition in English Drama of the Renaissance* (Univ. of Delaware, 1969).
The Downfall of Robert, Earl of Huntingdon, ed. G. C. Pittman (Univ. of Mississippi, 1967).
The Duchess of Malfi, ed. R. B. Carey (Univ. of Washington, 1969).
The Duchess of Suffolk, ed. R. A. Raines (Univ. of Delaware, 1968).
Edward III, ed. F. R. Lapides (Rutgers, The State Univ., 1966); ed. F. D. Horn (Univ. of Delaware, 1969).
The Empress of Morocco, ed. R. E. DiLorenzo (Univ. of Iowa, 1968). [In *An Edition of the Burlesque Plays of Thomas Duffett*.]
I The Fair Maid of the West, ed. B. Salomon (Tulane Univ., 1967).
The Family of Love, ed. A. Dillon (New York Univ., 1968).
The Female Virtuosos, ed. W. C. Wright (Univ. of Maryland, 1968). [Facsimile, with introd.]
A Fine Companion, ed. R. A. Sonnenshein (Northwestern Univ., 1968).
I and II Fulgens and Lucrece, ed. M. E. Moeslin (Univ. of North Carolina at Chapel Hill, 1968).
The Gentleman Dancing-Master, ed. D. S. Rodes (Stanford Univ., 1968).
The Ingratitude of a Commonwealth, ed. Ruth Ella McGugan (Univ. of Illinois, 1965). [In *Nahum Tate and the Coriolanus Tradition in English Drama with a Critical Edition of Tate's* The Ingratitude of a Common-wealth.]
I The Iron Age, ed. M. R. Evans (Florida State Univ., 1968).
James IV, ed. C. H. Stein (St. Louis Univ., 1968).
Jocasta, ed. C. F. W. Forssberg, Jr. (Vanderbilt Univ., 1968).
King John and Matilda, ed. J. O. Davis (Tulane Univ., 1969).
The Lady of May, ed. P. M. Murphy (Univ. of Wisconsin, 1969).
Look about You, ed. A. C. Begor (Harvard Univ., 1965).
A Looking Glass for London and England, ed. G. A. Clugston (Univ. of Michigan, 1966); ed. T. Hayashi (Kent State Univ.,

1968).
The Lost Lady, ed. D. F. Rowan (Univ. of New Brunswick, 1967).
Love in a Wood, ed. D. S. Rodes (Stanford Univ., 1968).
Love's Hospital, ed. J. L. Funston (Univ. of Arizona, 1968).
Love's Last Shift, ed. B. R. S. Fone (New York Univ., 1966); ed. M. Sullivan (Yale Univ., 1968).
A Mad World, My Masters, ed. M. J. Taylor (Univ. of Birmingham, 1963).
Misogonus, ed. L. E. Barber (Univ. of Arizona, 1967).
The Mock-Tempest, ed. R. E. DiLorenzo (Univ. of Iowa, 1968). [In *An Edition of the Burlesque Plays of Thomas Duffett.*]
Mucedorus, ed. N. P. Boyer (Univ. of Denver, 1969).
I and II Nature, ed. M. E. Moeslein (Univ. of North Carolina at Chapel Hill, 1968).
Nero, ed. S. J. Teller (Univ. of Illinois, 1967).
The Northern Middle English Harrowing of Hell Plays of the York and Towneley Cycles, ed. W. R. Cozart (Harvard Univ., 1963).
Parasitaster, or The Fawn, ed. D. A. Blostein (Univ. of Toronto, 1968). [In *The Comedy of John Marston with a Critical Edition of* The Fawn.]
The Parliament of Bees, ed. W. T. Locke III (Vanderbilt Univ., 1967).
A Play of Love, ed. F. E. LaRosa (Univ. of Illinois, 1968).
The Politician, ed. R. J. Fehrenbach (Univ. of Missouri, 1968).
I and II Promos and Cassandra, ed. G. W. Amos (Univ. of Arkansas, 1968).
Psyche Debauched, ed. R. E. DiLorenzo (Univ. of Iowa, 1968). [In *An Edition of the Burlesque Plays of Thomas Duffett.*]
The Puritan, ed. D. F. Kaiser (Univ. of Wisconsin, 1966).
The Queen's Arcadia, ed. L. H. Butrick (State Univ. of New York at Buffalo, 1968).
The Raging Turk, or Bajazet II, ed. D. Carnegie (Univ. Coll., London, 1967). [In *A Critical Edition of the Turkish Tragedies of Thomas Goffe.*]
Sir Giles Goosecap, ed. J. F. Hennedy (Univ. of Illinois, 1965).
The Sparagus Garden, ed. L. L. Panek (Kent State Univ., 1968).
Supposes, ed. C. F. W. Forssberg, Jr. (Vanderbilt Univ., 1968).
Tarugo's Wiles, ed. P. M. Park (Univ. of Pennsylvania, 1968).

[Facsimile, with introd. and notes.]

Time's Triumph; retitled *Time's Distractions* by D. W. Strommer in *A Critical Edition of an Anonymous, Titleless Play, Dated 1643, in British Museum MS. Egerton 1994* (Ohio State Univ., 1969).

The Two Maids of More-Clacke, ed. A. S. Liddie, Jr. (Rutgers, The State Univ., 1967).

The Two Merry Milkmaids, ed. G. H. Metz (Univ. of Pennsylvania, 1968).

The Virtuous Wife, or Good Luck at Last, ed. W. E. Carpenter, Jr. (Univ. of Kansas, 1967).

Wakefield Plays. Six plays (*The Annunciation, The Salutation, The Play of the Shepherds, The Flight of Joseph and Mary into Egypt, The Purification of Mary*, and *The Play of the Doctors*), ed. as *The Marian Pageants in the Towneley Cycle* by F. A. Hill (Univ. of Southern Mississippi, 1969).

The Wisdom of Doctor Dodypoll, ed. M. N. Matson (Northwestern Univ., 1967).

The Wise Woman of Hogsdon, ed. M. H. Leonard (Univ. of Southern California, 1967).

The Wives' Excuse, or Cuckolds Make Themselves, ed. R. R. Thornton (Univ. of Pennsylvania, 1966).

Women Beware Women, ed. J. R. Mulryne (St. Catherine's Coll., Cambridge, 1963).

The Young Admiral, ed. K. J. Ericksen (Rice Univ., 1967).

ADDENDA

1515. *Magnificence*. Limits: for 1515-1523 read *c*. 1504-1523 (Composition *c*. 1504 recently suggested.). [See L. Winser, 'Skelton's *Magnyfycence*', *Renaissance Quarterly*, XXIII (1970), 14-25.]

1549. *Add entire entry:*
Author: Ponet, John. Title: *The Unjust Usurped Primacy of the Bishop of Rome* (Trans. Ochino.) Limits: 1549. Type: Anti-Catholic Dialogue. Auspices: Closet. Earliest Texts: 1549**. Last Ed.: 1899[44].

1623. *Add entire entry:*
Author: Speed, John. Title: *Caps* (Characters include Cap, Hat, Head, Gown, Minerva, Mercury, etc.). Limits: 1623 (?). Type: Play with Mask. Auspices: St. John's Coll., Oxford. Earliest Texts: MS.

p. 210, entry 44. For Entry cancelled read C. E. Plumptre, ed., *The Tragedy by Bernardino Ochino*.

P. 227. Add: Ponet, or Poynet, John, Bishop of Winchester (1514?-1556), 1549 Supp. II.

P. 228. Speed, John. Add: 1623 Supp. II.

P. 293. Add, under Italian entries: Ochino, Bernardino (1487-1564), 1549 Supp. II.

P. 305. Hope. For The structure was still standing in 1683, but after 1617 had been used exclusively for bear-baiting read After 1617 the structure was used mostly for bear-baiting; it was pulled down in 1656. [See G. E. Bentley, *The Jacobean and Caroline Stage* (Oxford, 1941-1968), VI, 209-14.]

P. 305. Cockpit-in-Court. For *c.* 1632 read 1630. [See Bentley, *Jacobean and Caroline Stage*, VI, 270-72.]

List of Editions:

B. Individual Plays. Add: Lee, Nathaniel. *The Rival Queens*, ed. P. F. Vernon. Lincoln, Neb., 1970. (Regents Restoration Drama Ser.)

C. Facsimiles. Add, under Scolar Press:
Beaumont, F.; Fletcher, J. *Philaster* (1620).
Jonson, Ben. *The Alchemist* (1610).